WHAT
THE RIGHT HAND
KNOWS

FOR FRED—

Two shorten the road.

TABLE OF CONTENTS

Introduction by Richard Howard

III. Merely Shadows to the Unseen Grief

IV. Sweet the Wine, Sour the Payment

Acknowledgments

THE COST OF KNOWING

We ask whether the right hand knows what the left is doing. What strikes me as the pronounced virtue of Tom Healy's poems is that they let us know quite frankly what *both* hands *have done*—and what his heart, his head and his entire body have also done.

It is remarkable how many things in these clear and distinct poems—succinct acknowledgments of a life spent *spending*: time, money, and sex (if the Elizabethans called it *dying*, the Victorians had a less scary word for it in *spending*)—how many things still remain on Healy's hands.

How prodigal this new poet is in the acknowledgment of his expenditures, how prompt with an expensive opening line, one sure to cost him sooner or later:

> *My tongue remembers when I first tasted dirt ...*
> *What do we do when we hate our bodies?...*
> *After I found my blood in trouble ...*

Healy is ruinously generous with his own fallibility; how readily, for example, he reports in "Learning to Land" the insufficiency of his flying-lessons, blazoning for the first time in our poetry the mutilation of the landing-field into the beloved's overwhelming and helpless physique:

> *There was a slow lift*
> *from the body*
>
> *below me breathing—*
> *and the world unfolded*
>
> *and I let go.*

There are many projected as well as personal occasions for such failings: fables about such eminent others as Emerson, Stravinsky, even Lauren Bacall at Hotel Bel Air:

> *Here was someone for whom we felt*
> *even more deliciously bitter*
> *to see grown old than to see ourselves—*
> *foolish and not famous, but gloating to be guests*
> *the other guest couldn't chase away.*

When he can expose something about himself that is awful (and aweful), Healy's *franchise* is actually dire:

> *you say it was easier*
> *to fall for me thinking*
>
> *it was likely I'd be*
> *dead by now.*

And yet, there is a certain sorcery in this book. The elegantly stoic observations of this poet's gorgeously tattered life and loves reproach any guess at the speaker's age. Is it because he has (has always had?) so much conjuration in him that the wisdom seems so ageless, so innocent, in the welter of so much shameless acknowledgment? Well, when was the sibyl ever ashamed?

It gives me enormous pleasure as an anything but ageless reader to introduce and to celebrate these vivid poems. The smiles they compel are taut and tight-lipped, but the language conjuring that gratification is at once sumptuous and cost-effective, precise and loving.

—Richard Howard

All things are full of labour; man cannot utter it:
the eye is not satisfied with seeing, nor the ear
filled with hearing.

Ecclesiastes 1:8

I.

THE FIELD HATH EYEN

A LABOR OF MOLES

My tongue remembers
when I first
tasted dirt

and knew the thing
was no longer
to see myself

digging,
but furiously
to dig.

CHORUS OF ANIMALS

And on that farm, the pitch
and fever of pigs singing
cut by the crack and thud
of a .22 pistol when we shot and
slit them, boiled them in barrels.

Here a warble, there a hiss
of geese davening in the yard,
chasing dogs, pinching children
until we snapped their necks
and stacked them in a freezer.

Here a whimper, there a wailing
of cats begging milk,
coiled, wild and frightened,
stuffed in feedbags
and drowned in the pond.

Here a bellow, there a moan
of arthritic yellow cows,
dry, too old, pushed
and dragged to a truck
to the dog food factory.

And on that farm,
an auctioneer comes chanting
Ee—i—ee—i—o.
Here, there, a story abandoned—
tractors, all the animals, the sofa, the car.

And on that farm,
a family broken in empty June,
here, there,
no one singing
Ee—i—ee—i—o.

THE ANESTHESIOLOGIST'S KISS

He was the first
man I knew

with hair on his face.
I remember his beard

almost covering
his lips, then mine.

I remember
white cotton.

He held my chin
and pressed gently.

I tasted tobacco
and rain trickling

past the soft fears
of a five-year old

into the sturdy home
secrets become.

Oh, little rose.
Drift away.

ALARM

Excuse me, I said.
My room is on fire.
I'd been watching
the flame a long time.

A nervous little dog
sniffing the wall
until it found a spot
where it dug and grew.

The spark turned mean
and I turned cold.
I went down in slippers
to a table of trouble,

the family dinner
I wasn't having.
This time I smiled
while they ignored me.

Excuse me, I said,
and bit hard
into the rage
of no one listening

then took my slippers
out into the snow.

DEAD RECKONING

With the day still dark
and unbegun, full
of readiness to bleed,

I stood here
every morning and
commandeered

this small hill
just out of shouting distance
from the house

to call cows home
for milking.
And every morning

a solitary heron panicked
and rattled
up and out of fog

at the pond's edge
into that stand
of trees past

the border fence where
thunderclouds of lilac
were bulldozed

one summer
for the neighbor's
new, metal-sided barn,

where one Sunday
I walked in on him
standing in a wheelbarrow

fucking one of his heifers.
I was a boy
and I claimed

this small hill,
calling cows,
failing as her child.

MILK-TRUCK DRIVER

He looked like a dwarf
and walked like a goat.
He pissed in the gutter
and was hung like a horse.

He pranced then stood
and shook his mule,
handling himself
like a winning ticket.

Hunger was wired
tight to his eyes.
His teeth flickered—
blue-starting flames.

His face danced red.
I was twelve and yellow.
We were standing close
to the end of time.

He spoke and I
answered I'd be back
in a minute. His eyes
turned glassy with doubt.

But his hand still rocked,
calmly and glad, while
I fetched my brother
who came with a shovel.

He spat at the man—who
screamed—and he beat him.
So much blood.
But, oh, don't cry.

OH, HI DAD

I thought I had killed him.
But here he is,

come to life so quickly,
despite the scarce crop

of talk, how long
words went hungry,

the distance I'd driven
to dump his memory.

But here he is,
the fruit of famine,

an alphabet emptied
of ice or apology.

Look where it comes!
Here he is.

Taste and eat.
Smile and wave.

LOCAL OR STRANGE

They took the journey they'd talked about,
a Sunday drive on Tuesday.

They took lunch, took pictures,
took pleasure shaking their heads

when either lifted to light
the moth-flutter

of a neighbor's forgotten name,
wondering whatever happened

to her, to him,
the stories they'd fled.

Their past looked small,
almost comical and frail,

needing them
more than they were willing.

But they left it there,
both mother and son surprised

to settle for making it ordinary,
going back at safe speed

to a landscape invented
before safety—but

now too safe—maneuvering
along edges, the simplest

geometry of return,
only tracing circumferences,

marking the boundaries
of field and shelter.

And they left watching
their remembered selves waving,

as farmers do, whether cars
are local or strange.

MURMURATIONS IN THE WILDERNESS

I find you in places
I haven't attempted,

places where I hold
a stranger's hand.

I am a stranger.
No one has hands.

How things should be—
foolish, impossible,

workable enough.
As our mothers'

sons and almost
mothers to each other,

we've learned to nest
the twig, wattle,

binding of words,
into safety—

as if some small
wound has healed.

We almost
taste the scar.

II.

THEIR OWN PHYSICIANS

WHAT THE RIGHT HAND KNOWS

I am not in stereo.
Deaf in one ear,

I am unable
with any accuracy

to pinpoint clamor
and quiet.

Argument reaches me
only on my left or

marching down
the center of the street

cleared
of other traffic.

I lose the background,
the sotto voce.

I lose scratch,
whisper, rain,

white noise, color
if it's muted,

the good gossip
unless I turn to it.

Stories must
circle west

toward twilight.
I have no east.

I learned this
on an ordinary afternoon,

my parents fighting,
torching one another,

and the only place
to run for cover

was standing there,
covering my ears.

But my right hand slipped—
to nothing.

Nothing?
I rolled up the gates,

brought my fingers
flat again, lifted

one, then the other.
Both hands. Neither.

I don't know why I didn't
cry or

tell anyone
the sound wasn't working.

Suddenly strange,
hearing and not—

I kept the sugar taste
of that secrecy

well-hidden
until eventually

Armstrong
landed on the moon

and our family's first
color console

broadcast the Earth
reflected in the bubble

over the astronaut's face—
itself another

television
attached to the body

of the best father
of all possible worlds.

Did you know,
I said to my mother,

that the moon's dark side
has no sound?

MY ORBIT

I spar with a boxer
who'd destroy me
if this were anything

like fighting.

But on this wood floor
I am what I pretend to be—

my hook blisters,
my jabs blind.

I am the sun

in a Copernican circuit
of sweat and bruise.

Enter my orbit
at risk to your own.

My wild swings
will scorch your fields
and bleed the sky.

Defend yourself.
Defend me.

LAMENTS AND RIDDLES

i.

Unlike mint, you don't
stay on the tongue.

What haunts the mouth
is not rage's sugar

dissolving, but the taste
of us, evaporating.

ii.

Someone has toyed
with the history.

Was it you?
Events rearranged,

my good dolls broken.
Who took liberties,

sat in the chair,
decided not to eat?

Who left warmth
in these sheets?

Everything here
was to stay cold.

iii.

It's called sistering
the joist

side by side
our lumber

nailed by need
by fear

of the roof's weight
(Give me your hand—)

what slips
what termites devour

this diminished wood
will hold

LIVING ON SOMEONE ELSE'S MONEY

What it means is flowers
always on the table,

flowers faking it gracefully
a few more days

in collectible glass and
silver ways of holding

colors no longer living,
flowers you didn't

choose yourself, names
you didn't learn,

extravagances you don't
admit you take for granted

or sometimes even tire of—
flowers and this panic.

YOU TWO?

We offer in evidence
our grocery list—

its crabbed scribbled
archeology of hunger

shorthand reckoning
of how we've settled

arguments
whether the week

augured skim milk
or vodka

cantaloupe or ice cream
little proclamations

smudged on the back
of an envelope

his marks and mine
a currency

the exchange of whim
and sustenance

an account not just
of comfort and ordinary

cravings but how
we've construed

the necessities
of rescue and surrender

AN ACT OF FORBEARANCE

i.

You're the type
who'd murder.
I'm the one
who eyes
his own wrists.
Should we wed
and spend life
thwarting
one another?

ii.

Compare apples
and oranges.

Compare fiction
and breathing.

One peeled,
one bitten.

Which, my spider,
is which?

We swing
in the threads

of this web
waiting

for sting,
for struggle.

iii.

Consider this.
Consider clay
where there
was once a field.

Consider
what it would
have been for us
to flower—

or stealing
the work
of another verb,
to weed.

iv.

I have my doubts
about the alphabet
bending to our will
like spoons.

We're the ones
always following
like dogs
and their tongues,

fetching for letters,
playing dead
across sentences,
working sad eyes.

Pity me
in the pound.

THE GREEN STREET MORTUARY BAND

It wasn't really our intention
to parade behind

the tinny music,
shadow the slovenly

drummers and trumpeter,
the slow drift

of confetti
blessed away

by bored little girls
riding slow in the family car.

But we got giddy,
drunk on good weather,

echoes in the street,
the oom-pa-pa

tugging our sleeve.
Pindar said

there'd be
horses in heaven.

He assured the crowd
we'd always need

what we have now—
we'd be safe

in the ways
we think we must travel.

And here we are,
thieves on foot.

MIRROR, MIRROR

What do we do when we hate our bodies?
A good coat helps.
Some know how to pull off a hat.

And there are paints, lighting, knives, needles,
various kinds of resignation,
the laugh in the mirror, the lie

of saying it doesn't matter.
There is also the company we keep:
surgeons and dermatologists,

faith healers and instruction-givers,
tailors of cashmere and skin
who send their bills for holding

our shame-red hands, raw
from the slipping rope,
the same hands with which we tremble

ever so slightly, holding novels in bed,
concentrating on the organization
of pain and joy

we say is another mirror,
a depth, a conjure in which we might meet
someone who says touch me.

III.

MERELY SHADOWS
TO THE UNSEEN GRIEF

PHOCION'S WIFE

He failed
and they wanted him dead.

They made a fire.
Burned him.

But that was not enough.
So they abandoned him

unburied, scattered,
refused rest.

When did the thought
occur to her?

Was it a promise
or something understood

at the strike
of tinder

as flames reached up
and carried off

his scream,
cinders lifting

him calling
her name?

A child at play again,
she churned

the blackened silt of him
into water, fizz

of a few last
embers.

Her hands, blistered
from having gathered him,

lifted the jar of thick paste.
More water.

She stirred and drank,
drank deeply.

It must have taken
all day.

Is this love—
the taste of ash

and smoke,
the grit of bone—

becoming
his tomb?

ZOO STORY

A great wooden cage hung
from St. Mark's campanile,
a little zoo for prisoners,
a nuisance for the keepers
of the piazza contending

with the huddled filth
of drunks, foreigners, thieves
they hoisted up into
mockery, sun-scorch, rain,
barely out of reach of the crowd.

The captives pissed and shat
on their tormenters,
who cursed and laughed below
and threw back the sour
mess of living that fell,

jabbing the criminal feet
with their torches, while
a few crippled steps away
were other, opulent moods—
candle-dark, mosaics, gold,

hymns in smoke and Latin.
If you weren't out pissing
down on someone's head,
you could stand the hour
and sing your hungry song.

DOORS SHOULD ALWAYS SWING *INTO* A ROOM

—Edith Wharton

Be vigilant with
the color of paint,
the pattern in which

tiles are set, the height
from which curtains dive,
how curve of light meets

curve of plastered wall,
how restrained a stitch
the carpets require

on which so much quiet
ambition will rush
in slippered bliss,

and the proper
arrangement of sofa, table,
object and chair

to play the cold-blood
of hide and seek
and disappear

GIOCONDA ON SEVENTH AVENUE

She entered the diner as if
many men had rowed
to bring her here.

We became the scenery
she needed, the backdrop
and the eyes within it.

What does the beauty
of a stranger mean?
There must be some physics

of emotion and need,
a law governing the lyrical
proximity of moving bodies,

to explain what draws us closer—
native and intruder—to the hour
we'll be eclipsed or saved.

AMONG THE MISSING

i. Mr. Stravinsky

He said his music was best understood
by children and animals.

He said
he was an animal
dying

from people's stares into his cage
at the zoo—

desperate eyes hunting his fame,
murdering idiots
trying to flush something out of him

as if there were something
to see.

And the dirty secret was
there was
something to see,

something
he himself was hunting,

sounds that moved
in stealth in his mind,
sounds he knew had shape.

He saw their shadows.

He saw the mocking breath
of panthers
that left no tracks,

running wild, diving
into black water

somewhere within him
eluding any torch or snare—

no trophies to haul back
other than anguish
at what escaped.

He cursed the cunning of music,

its willingness to drown
rather than be
made slave to clarity.

Mr. Stravinsky, the world still riots.
Something is out there.

Tell us what it is.
We want it.
We will kill for it.

The animal thinking.
Children singing.

ii. Emerson's Umbrella

A friend's funeral.

It was raining.
His coat was wet and too thin.
He was cold.
No hat.

He stood with the others
in solemn huddle
but his words walked away.

Names slid from him,
dripping down
whisker, shoulder, boot to grass,
run-off of mind, unminded
into mud.

He stood
refusing to shiver,

stepping inside himself,
pacing in front of coals
slowed from burning to glow

in some interior place.

Something like a crow
was just out of reach
out the window,

a crow that might
spread wing over his shoulders
to shelter him.

It was a word.

He stepped back out
into the rain
where he was all along.

He could see the word.

It was tethered to him
by string.

He tugged at it.

It would not come.
Eight stubborn letters
of temporary shelter.

He grabbed
at the rain.

His friends
looked up at his clenched
angry hand.

"I need," he said,
"what strangers take away."

THE PEACOCKS OF CUERNAVACA

I don't trust these birds—
the larcenous eyes,
that strut of deception.

Their gorgeous hesitation is a ruse.
I'll bet they have
hollow fingers and string

hiding under their feathers—
they're puppeteers
tugging a choreography of calm

out of our shame at having
no color, and the awkward
emptiness of our own hands.

But out there late, in the crooks
of bordering eucalyptus
it's them (I know it is)

gathered for a nightshift
of hideous rasps
and caterwauls,

spitting into the cage
around my sleep, mocking me
with their evil little fists.

Come here
you damn birds.
Give me those hands.

THE ONLY FRUIT

Spring 1999 Hotel Bel Air

You know something?
These strawberries look great,
but they're hard, unsuccessful things.
I can't eat them.
I'll have the kiwi. Kiwi is better.
Not the prettiest, but smart.
The juice is good.

And then there was a pause.

Everyone anywhere nearby luxuriated in the discomfort,
hesitating, waiting to hear that

Those are not kiwi, Miss Bacall.
They're pears.

And then, another pause.
A pause that was all hers.

Oh.

A pause.
A breath.
A sigh.

Is nothing . . . ever right?
Go.
Make someone miserable until I get something else.

—the saying of which caused her almost to smile at herself.

Leaning in from her chaise in the shade of an olive tree,
cocooned in a cable knit sweater,
perfumed in the poolside eucalyptus air,
emerging from somewhere small and pubescent,
here was fame almost smiling.

Here was someone for whom we felt
even more deliciously bitter
to see grown old than to see ourselves—
foolish and not famous, but gloating to be guests
this other guest couldn't chase away.

And then, ignoring almost everyone and everything
while paying exquisite attention to all and all,
she turned her celebrity vaguely in the direction
of the handsome Mexican pool boy hovering,
almost whispering that famous bark of hers,

Well, then.
Do you have—I admit I'm a little
seduced by the name,
a bit wily if you ask me—
do you have any
clementines?

LEARNING TO LAND

The world folded
and I let go.

Cuffed, shoved and
kicked down,

my single-engine Cessna
dropped through

black-boot
clouds and rain.

Though I was
mugged and tumbled,

it's actually difficult
for a small plane

not to fly.
The propeller lashed

the air and the plane
jumped

through the window
of late afternoon,

leveling off
a couple thousand feet

above the earth's belly,
its easy rise and fall

against a ribcage
of trees and road.

There was a slow lift
from the body

below me breathing—
the world unfolded

and I let go.

IV.

SWEET THE WINE,
SOUR THE PAYMENT

THE VIEW FROM HERE

Giotto drew a perfect circle
with one quick
turn of coal.

The shape
of astonishment,
forever's empty frame,

a coin on the tongue,
how our eyes never are.
But relax, love,

into this world we're finding
and the perfect hurt
of how it turns.

THE METAPHYSICS OF BEING WELL-MANNERED

The way you eat pizza—
fork and knife,
cloth napkin,

making careful cuts
in the direction
of all four winds—

is black tie in the desert,
a blizzard lit by candles.
The way you eat pizza

a lullaby among jackals,
prolegomenon to peace—
the night's hunger call

suddenly so hushed
in admiration
of the way you eat pizza,

cicadas forget to stutter
and the moon's thirst
is well-said.

BODY ELECTRIC

i.

You spit in my face
and I laugh.

You demand
I call you sir, yes, sir,

and I keep
getting it wrong.

The thrum of current
burns best

when we just
lie reading,

and talk
is such better sex—

gossip
and Henry James.

ii.

I ask a boy
held in by some

anger or sadness
if he has seen

the moon tonight
floating almost

astonishingly
full and low,

a circle of wet paint
patching the vacancy

we hover under.
The boy is bored

by approaches like this
and doesn't look

anywhere as he answers.
Has he seen

the moon?
Only from a distance.

iii.

Fiddlestick legs, carpet-back,
garbage-bag belly,

a man my father's age
who calls himself Count—

Count O'Brien of Ireland,
take off your clothes,

the knee-high socks
and double-breasted blazer,

your nelly snigger of brass
and blue, buttoned up

and pocket-silked.
Close your eyes.

Bite the pillow.
Your belt is in my hands.

NO FEAR OF FIRE

We are trees

and confess to nothing
in this ruckus of leaves
or its balancing catechism
of no sound.

No burden of trails,
no forestry
scratched into this hill,
nothing startled
from our underbrush.

Just the sun's unrooted gaze
jealous our thirst
has such glad color
and no fear of fire.

Let it come.

Rain will also come
and we are many.

And when questions come
from angrier landscapes,
answers will echo

in the laughter swirling
through our standing here

in promiscuous wind.

TABLE OF SPIDERS

We used to kiss
in greeting one another—
summer in our touch,

warm weather
and bare feet
while we sat

in the rocking chairs
of each other's
moods.

Now we're spiders
at a communal table,
trapped indoors,

spinning exaggeration
and making fun
of prey, afraid

someone is coming
with an upended broom.
We get drunk

and rage, wasting time
competing
for the younger,

prettier kids
who stumble in
pretending to admire us,

weeping like Alcibiades—
the room afloat
in a teaspoon of their tears.

VOODOO

Everyone is so involved
keeping track of my pills:

my husband, his secretary,
our protective housekeeper

who counts them out in Creole,
numbering a scattered universe

of nebulae clustered on the bed
when she helps me pack

for Florida or days
an even greater distance

lays claim to. She says
it's like the rosary,

counting and whispering,
and she teaches me words

for purple, white, yellow, a shock
of orange, two different blues,

and a curse on one that's striped
turquoise and kelly green.

FOR RENT

One we love is hurt,
faltered by weight,

his own neglect
and ours. But sleep,

vegetables, short walks
outside to knock

a little sunshine
off the path and

stretch the limbs—
these won't work.

They just lead
to the logic of failure,

the panic that mind
is not enough.

Better to pretend
we can hold out

long enough for the skeptic's
shop to get set up

where we could rent
bodies for ourselves

or think we did,
and glory in being

or wondering whether
we're brains in a vat—

once in a while
drying the thing off,

snapping it into
a handsome skull,

getting ourselves
a good fit frame

and putting our rented
tongue to work

on the salt
of someone else's skin.

It would be enough
to feel a little wine

ride down our throats,
to dance and even twist

our ankles, to fall
and feel just enough

pain to take ourselves
seriously again before

the rental was up
when we could blissfully

go back to our neglect
and our reading.

BEEKEEPER

My arms are out, sweet chariot.
Swing low and pull me in.

Take me where the vanished
honeybees muster,

to the nectar colony
of hummingbirds and party boys

skirring and spinning
on some curve in space.

The cracks in things
have been filled

with television and cement
and the rules for dancing

long ago turned over
to the arbitration of ants.

Convince me
to bring the honeybees

home
or leave me there

armored in the swarm
of their wings.

HERE AND NOW

After I found
my blood in trouble

I could hear its rapid
underground current swell—

terrorists setting tributaries aflame
at low tide.

And I could see
the agony of other rivers—

how they burned, blistered,
wasted into dry beds.

That was the weather.
And now?

A purple calm.
Only the barely surviving

echo of hysteria.
There are few birds

and no river dolphins
and it's unwise to swim.

But these are modest,
local toxins—

the war itself
has floated past

leaving something
like ordinary days.

Here, now—
the breeze of survival.

In this shallow place,
in shade and therapy,

the task is to remember
the troubled blood of others

and not remember
the bliss of deeper water.

A POSSUM ENTERING THE ARGUMENT

We're talking about
when we met
and you say

it was easier
to fall for me thinking
(I'll remember

this pause)
it was likely I'd be
dead by now.

Talking. Falling.
Thinking. Waiting …
Have I

undone
what you've tried to do?
You say no.

You say the surprise
of still being
is something

being built—
the machine of our living,
this saltwork of luck,

stylish, safe,
comfortable and
unintended.

Meanwhile, I haven't
had the opportunity
to tell you, but

our lovely little dog
has just killed
a possum.

Maybe it's unfair,
a possum entering
the argument here.

But I lay it down
before us:
because an ugly

dying possum
played dead
and didn't run,

its dubious cunning
was brought to an end
outside our door

by our brutal, beautiful
and very pleased
little dog.

So how do I say
that this is not
about death or sadness

or even whether
you really
first loved me

waiting, thinking
I'd be
dying young?

It's just that
standing there
a few minutes ago

holding a dead possum
by its repellent
bony tail,

I was struck by how
eerily pleased I was
to be a spectator

to teeth, spit,
agony and claw,
feeling full of purpose,

thinking how different
in our adversaries
we are from possums.

We try love—
the fist of words,
their opening hand.

And whether we play
dead or alive,
our pain, the slow

circulation of happiness,
our salt and work,
the stubborn questions

we endlessly
give names to
haunt us with choice.

ACKNOWLEDGMENTS

My great thanks to John Ashbery for his collage on the cover
and to Richard Howard for introducing me ... to new worlds
of thinking, reading, and writing.

The genealogy of my debts and gratitude is too long to name
the many other names. But I sing of my family and friends,
even if it's silent.

✩

I am grateful to the editors of the following journals
and anthologies who have published poems from this collection:

*BOMB; Drunken Boat; LIT; Open City; The Paris Review; Salmagundi;
Washington Square; The Yale Review, Aroused: An Anthology of
Erotic Writing,* Karen Finley, editor; and *Tigertail: A Florida Poetry
Anthology,* Campbell McGrath, editor.

✩

My section titles are thefts:

"The field hath eyen, and the wood hath ears." *The Knightes Tale,*
line 1524

"Those whose suffering is due to love are, as we say of certain
invalids, their own physicians." *Within a Budding Grove,* p. 578,
Moncrieff translation

"And these external manners of lament / Are merely shadows to
the unseen grief," *Richard II,* 4.1.294-7

"Sweet the wine, sour the payment." Irish proverb

Tom Healy lives in New York and Miami. His poems and essays have appeared in *BOMB, The Paris Review, Salmagundi, Tin House, The Yale Review,* and other journals. He studied at Harvard and Columbia.